NUTS & BOLTS OF
CHRISTIANITY

JAMES L. FARRELL

American Literary Press, Inc.
Five Star Special Edition
Baltimore, Maryland

Nuts & Bolts of Christianity

Library of Congress
Cataloging-in-Publication Data
ISBN 1-56167-890-2

Library of Congress Card Catalog Number:
2004195077

Published by

American Literary Press, Inc.
Five Star Special Edition
8019 Belair Road, Suite 10
Baltimore, Maryland 21236

Manufactured in the United States of America

How to dedicate this writing? There are so many candidates: wife, son, daughter, brother, sister, co-worker, friend ⋯ . None would object, though, to the following decision — **To** *the disadvantaged. Any profits due the author from this writing will be donated to the Salvation Army.*

CONTENTS

PREFACE

This short book consists of 52 reflections, one for each week of the year. I would have compiled one for each day but I don't know 365 things (it was a stretch to get as high as 52). While intended to be helpful it makes no pretense of authoritativeness. Myriad topics are pondered, in varying length, assembled from multiple unrelated segments including

- · influential events
- · contemplations
- · anecdotes overheard
- · "psychic" energy – *not* supernatural; more like a very weak TV signal
- · etc.

Not all of the items are original. Most are taken from my experience and observations, but some were borrowed from others' seeming to contain information that is important to spread. All of the selections offer some chance to help figure out "how things work" in the (often mysterious-to-the-point-of-confusing) world. Some of my experiences that led to entries herein were trying – even grueling; I'm convinced they needed to be. While images conveyed by "nuts-&-bolts" imply a mundane perspective (and many excerpts came from routine experiences), obviously there is heavy influence of an engineering interpretation and of Christianity; an author's background will come through the writings. That is not by any means intended to exclude non-Christians; there are various ongoing efforts toward bringing different faiths together, and I definitely endorse those.

My observation at the dawn of the third millennium A.D. is that, although Anne Frank was right (most people are good), a small fraction who *aren't* good can now threaten the safety of millions on this planet. How can control be taken away from those irresponsible ones? Christianity offers answers but many shy away from Christianity for reasons that aren't valid. Admittedly there are *in*valid reasons – preachers motivated primarily by money, "Christians"who claim a monopoly on God, presumptuously consign others to hell, or assume other authority they don't have, etc. – but, just as we must resist bad advice in any situation, we need to rely on our own judgments for this crucial issue.

The *Inventor* of Christianity is the real Authority, not anyone who misquotes Him. He personified tact, patience, gentle persuasion, inescapably flawless logic. He didn't act superior, play politics, ram the facts down everyone's throat, nor do dozens of other things that turn so many away. In fact He counteracted those who did play those games. He's the God of those who don't feel important, don't act important – the ones who just try to meet their obligations and carry out their responsibilities as best they can. That includes all of us who fail, as long as we keep trying. Most of us aren't authorities but workers. In a lot of cases we feel as if our work doesn't make any difference. Hey c'mon, understand: that could be proof of your validity; you're opposite to the puffed-up pretender! If readers forget all but one thing from this writing, let this be the thing remembered: *never quit*. It really is true that many winners are former losers who fell flat on their faces a thousand times – and got up a thousand and one times.

Clearly all limitations and any errors here are entirely the fault of the author and must not be attributed to Christianity nor to other Christians.

THAT'S CHRISTIANITY

"My brother was in the room. He looked at me and said, 'We are Christians. We've got to go help him out,' and I said, 'Right.' Then he went and got his keys."

— *Lei Yuille*

Those words aren't yet carved in marble somewhere at the nation's capitol, but I'll do what I can to help immortalize them.

The place was Los Angeles, not long after the time of the Rodney King episode. When justice is not served — and hasn't been served so many times before — it may not take much to generate a mob enraged at the outcome. That happened in that city, at a time when rapid demographic changes had already made the place a tinderbox ready to ignite without much provocation. A hapless driver, at the wrong place at that time, was chosen as a sacrificial lamb by that mindless mob.

Almost by definition, a mob resists any appeal to reason. Anyone who risks going against the will of a mob risks his or her life. Some persons are willing to do that, for no reason other than a fundamental conviction that it's the right thing to do. Lei Yuille and her brother had no idea that anyone would ever notice their heroic bravery fueled by sheer idealism. They initiated a sequence of events leading to the rescue of that hapless driver.

I won't even attempt to add anything to the account. *That's* Christianity.

1

James L. Farrell

HOW MANY RESCUES?

The gas tank was still half full. No need to add more right away; in fact, not until the next day. Minneapolis was far behind, and I could reach Milwaukee without stopping at all. It's always more efficient to fill up when the tank is far down − then it doesn't have to be done as often. Ah well, I pulled into the station anyway for no apparent conscious reason. It was unusual for me to do that.

From a few steps beyond the gas pump there was a very loud noise. Turning around I saw an enormous tractor-trailer that stopped just short of where I was standing after it collided with whatever structure halted its movement. Witnesses stated that it had been weaving across the highway at about 90 miles per hour. Glad I stopped exactly when and where I did.

During the years since that Friday night there were more, many more, rescues. Some were just as potentially threatening and many were just as seemingly improbable. On a Saturday night in early January 1981 I was at the "Top of the World" restaurant atop the World Trade Center when a foreign airliner, essentially blinded by fog, very nearly collided with the building. That time it would have been accidental − still, without action by an alert air traffic controller, I would have been gone.

After adding up just the fraction of rescues I remember (dozens, not even counting the ones that happened without my awareness of them), the thought occurred to me: How did I survive? Furthermore, how did I even avoid making a mess out of my life? While we're at it, there's sight — my rare type of glaucoma was seen by dozens of nationally recognized experts when I was in my 20's. Consensus: my sight would be lost. Decades later, it hasn't happened. My case now has world-class experts at Johns Hopkins Wilmer Institute mystified (including experts who inserted a plastic lens in one eye that was useless; now that's my best eye — I use it to read without glasses). Why was I able, long ago, to find Dr. Julian Goldberg who managed my case so brilliantly? Also, while questions are flowing, how did all my life's fragments hold together after all the disruptions?

If this were a joke book I'd attempt to express some comical way of assuming full credit for myself. That's not what's going on here, though. It couldn't be more clear: years ago, experts from coast to coast didn't expect my sight to last, and I didn't save myself from that truck nor that airliner. If the other rescues were described on this page, the same conclusion would be just as clear. There is no need to be preoccupied with details of all those incidents at this point. More important is one intriguing issue: When dozens of highly improbable events all turn out successful, then either of two facts must be recognized as true:
  · an accumulation of events, against odds that are astronomical when the combination is considered, just happened — *or*
  · Supernatural help was at work.

I'm grateful for all the rescues — and grateful for the feeling of gratitude.

OF the CHRISTIANS, BY a CHRISTIAN, and FOR the CHRISTIANS

As we recall the dawn of the 3rd millennium, let's fast-forward the tape another hundred years: Happy new year twenty-*one* hundred.   The sportscaster is announcing the next fight as the Christians square off against ... the Christians! Wait a minute; did I say a fight? On second thought, make that a free-for-all. Furthermore, there are no teams.   Each individual Christian represents a separate and unique sect. There are now as many denominations as there are Christians. What was that about scattering the flock? What flock? Oh, for the good old days (around the year 2000) when there were "only" between 400 and 500 denominations. Actually was that the ideal? Christ never said "there shall be 400 folds and 400 shepherds" – with each one claiming that the other 399 don't know what they're doing.

The good news is that the scattering process won't really go all the way to that limit; in fact, there's a promise of one fold and one Shepherd. Still, there's enough disunity now to place unnecessary obstacles along the path toward transition to that unified state – and real misfortune is manufactured in the delaying process.

Now, looking back from the year 2100, how did it all come to this? Was it merely one facet of modern life reflecting another? By the year 2000 it was already clear, after all, that society was fragmented and growing increasingly more fragmented. In some ways, even *progressively* more fragmented. It wasn't just the realization – since government plus business plus seemingly all other institutions were splintered, it was

4

logical to expect the same in churches – we already figured out that much. The problem was that forces were firmly in place to magnify that trend even further. All the more reason for Christians from all walks of life to find common ground for cooperation. Uh, I guess some of us missed it so far. Let's do a post-mortem on how; maybe if we understand how so many of us became divided in the past, we can move toward unity sooner in the future.

We can start with one of the bright spots in the picture, *i.e.*, the emergence of non-denominational / inter-denominational / multi-denominational Christian groups sprouting up throughout the U.S. toward the end of the 20th century. Beaucoup cross-fertilization of ideas, beaucoup positive philosophy, beaucoup songs, beaucoup uplifting of spirit – especially while communicating about issues where Christians of different backgrounds agree. Communicating about issues where Christians of different backgrounds *differ* was trickier. Not a bad thing to delve into, certainly; in fact, it's necessary sooner or later. What complicates the operation is the tendency, in some of us, to insist that our own approach – with every detail in precise conformance to our own individual specification – absolutely and obviously represents the only valid way to practice Christianity. With that subject raised, we can return to a late-1990's vantage point.

The item just mentioned has ramifications beyond our immediate frontier. Although it may be easy to filter out some of the more obvious misrepresentations of Christianity (*e.g.*, 'churches' that exist as a tax dodge; those indifferent to the plight of the disadvantaged; those preaching the message 'Just send money' ⋯), there are serious-minded Christians who unwittingly drive people away. If we invoke the name of Christ, insisting that He is on our side – and thus anyone who disagrees with us is hopelessly lost – then we are practicing something very different from Christianity. Most scriptural passages describing people's encounters with Jesus show Him to be exceptionally tactful; gentle to the extent of meekness. While a firm and uncompromising stance was taken in some instances, accompanied by an unmistakable reproach of those being addressed, let's remember that Christ had to authority to do that; He had the insight to read minds and hearts. If we assume that same authority and insight for ourselves, we risk misquoting the Truth that we claim to be sharing.

Note that the above observation offers a judgment about the competence – not the moral character or integrity – of the offenders. Sincerity, zeal, energy – none of that is missing; but the consequences of these actions should prompt a humble reaction, not a proud one. If we speak with discordant voices within the Christian community, we aren't helping the move toward an eventual one-fold-and-one-Shepherd condition.

With all that stated, it must be acknowledged that some groups call themselves "churches" solely for tax-dodging purposes while others teach beliefs that clearly and fundamentally contradict Scripture. That of course can't be accommodated. No one said this would be easy; we leave resolution of all that to the appropriate authorities. In view of the track record thus far, that may sound defeatist. It isn't; there's a promise that this will happen.

THE BEST DECISIONS COME from the BEST INFORMATION

A tank commander's position offers the best available view of conditions. Because of superior information, he has access to controls that can override crew command signals. Common sense; if you know more you can do better. If that's true on a mundane level, how much more does it hold for a Supreme Commander with unlimited intelligence?

First let's combine all that we value into one big collection, including the state of our relationships plus knowledge plus talents plus opportunities plus material wealth plus whatever else fits. Everything that's "mine" actually belongs to the Source Who generously gave everything listed in my name. Other creatures aren't entitled to take away what's "mine" but God does have that right. No exceptions, no claims to right of ownership, no conditions (no nuttin'). Whatever stewardship responsibilities I have can prompt me to action – fair enough. Any action carried out though, however informed it may seem, must be recognized as a guess on my part – and therefore subject to Commander override.

Is there a practical application for this concept? Here's one: unknown to many of us, there are some multimillionaires today who make enormous charitable donations. If more of the overprivileged saw the same light, a bigger reduction could be made in the poverty and misery across this planet. If *everyone* saw that light, that misery could be minimized.

OK, so that just stated the obvious. There are times when stating and restating the obvious can be justified. This is one of those times. The severity of unbalance

7

in the distribution of the earth's resources – and the consequences – demand *re*balancing.

Rachel Carson's *Silent Spring* singlehandedly changed the course of environmental damage with a highly informed dire warning. In roughly the same time period, a noted economist (Barbara Ward) issued comparably urgent warnings about exploiting weak economic power of underdeveloped countries. Unfortunately those latter warnings went largely unheeded. That would not have happened with a Christian approach to stewardship. An alarming fraction of the earth's population is in misery while too many of us, seemingly unaware, continue to chase meaningless fads and other forms of waste. When we get hit over the head (think 9/11/01), we still don't change our priorities to a top-side-up orientation. If that's been stated a thousand times, state it a thousand more times. State it a million more times – maybe then enough people will react to it *and retain their reaction.* That hasn't happened yet.

WHAT'S the MISSION ?

A widespread and increasingly popular procedure is to write a mission statement. The intent is to provide a specific definition of purpose (or in some cases multiple purposes, possibly with priorities indicating the relative importance of each). Clarification of purpose first in the mind is then expected to influence actions that are likely conducive to realizing at least some of the stated goals. Covey's seven habits and all that.

The custom clearly makes sense for organizations – so much sense, in fact, that it might often seem difficult to justify *not* having a mission statement for an organization. It is not surprising that the practice is also followed by individuals. If you or I have written a mission statement, it might enhance the probability that we can achieve our objectives. If nothing else it can be an antidote to aimlessness. In *Open Secrets* by Alice Munro, characters yearn for "a destiny to submit to ⋯ something that claims us, anything, instead of such flimsy choices, arbitrary days."

OK, so what's my excuse for not having one?

We all know that every individual is different, ("what works for one may or may not apply to another ⋯ " etc.). As with everyone else, there are a few (very few) things I do much better than others – and many things I don't do well at all. I've experienced enough success in a few different areas (on an intermediate scale, of course, not on a grand scale). The results leave me with a sense that specific outcomes, while not arbitrary, are somewhat open to alternatives. If I mentally assign rigid priority sequences to my favorite five activities, who's to guarantee that the order will be right? It then seems possible that efforts could be misdirected because of inaccurate ranking of preferences.

Here's one possible reaction to that: I ask God to define my mission statement, and to put me on track towards satisfying it. It's still my responsibility, of course, to remain alert for opportunities and to supply my part of the effort when needed. It's not random but it's not rigid either. We can try to work toward the right direction and still stay adaptable. Step-by-step along the way, asking for guidance with each step.

THE PROBLEMS AREN'T NEW

We read it all the time. In the USA today, values are down, people are unhappy, injustice is everywhere, corruption is rampant, ⋯ . Hey, wait a minute – that isn't news. One of the prominent scandals dominating the news for a couple of years (Watergate; abuse of authority at the highest possible level of power) happened during the early 1970s. Even older than that were lesser-known examples of big business milking profits from Great Society programs intended to help the disadvantaged. That led George Romney to offer this recommendation at the end of his stint as first-ever Secretary of Housing and Urban Development: abolish the department. That happened even after it had been common knowledge, before initiation of those programs in the 1960s, that success could become evident only a generation later – and then only if they were administered correctly.

Other events, also decades old, include revealing statements by individuals who were prominent at the time. Senator Everett McKinley Dirksen, in a commencement address, described the world about to be inherited by the new graduates: "Your elders have made a mess of it." Defense attorney F. Lee Bailey observed that conviction or acquittal *has nothing to do with* guilt or innocence in a criminal trial between "gladiator lawyers." Probably less conspicuous, but equally startling, was a breakthrough report from a leading cancer research institute – a disease was reportedly "cured" by removing spots that had been painted on the skin of a laboratory animal. Also from the medical profession we have examples such as widespread mistreatment in homes for the aged (a problem much older than its comparatively recent exposure). And who can forget the widespread overcharging for commonplace items in the defense industry?

These are just representative samples – add your own case to the list – but the point has been made. With abuse glaringly visible in every direction it might be useful to nominate the worst industry of all (my vote: the down-is-up/west-is-east/good-is-bad/bad-is-good entertainment business). More urgent than assignment of guilt, though, is focus of attention on a crucial question: Why couldn't we correct misdeeds that were so obvious for so long? When *every* profession needs reform it's time for overhaul ("the system is broken"). Consider how our social conditions have worsened in the past 25-year period – can we allow that much more deterioration during the next? How much weaker can we become before we're due for Commander override?   Would anyone expect that ride to be smooth?   We are like characters in an old Russian novel, seeing how far we can lean out the window without falling.

Historically, collapse of a powerful nation has been preceded by widespread Godlessness and corruption, combined with unwarranted complacency ("it can't happen here").

All of this lends urgency for correction – from within ourselves. Still, despair isn't the answer – and neither is anarchy; reform is definitely possible. What we need right now is the will.

AS THE INSECT FLIES

Here's where the control *isn't*: it isn't with us. Consider two scenarios, starting out the same but with two very different conclusions —

Version A
At a cocktail party your attention is drawn to a member of the opposite sex, wearing a striking white blazer, standing across the room. As you search your mind for a means of becoming introduced, that individual starts crossing the room in a path near you. At the same time a friend walks toward you and compliments your work published in a recent book. To your delight, *the one* overhears the compliment and interjects a comment: "You wrote a book on that? I've always wanted to know more about that topic." You manage somehow to keep a straight face and, from outward appearances, to maintain your composure through a determined effort to appear calm while answering.

Version B
Same cocktail party, same knockout individual in the white blazer, same friend. As that friend reaches a position next to you, air currents direct an insect's flight path right into your eye. Just before your friend has a chance to mention your recent publication, you reflexively move your hand toward your eye. But you forgot that there is a glass of burgundy wine in that hand. The burgundy wine is spilled all over that white blazer. Conversation aborted.

Could either of these outcomes occur without any intervention in the way of anyone's free will? Yes. Are the air current patterns under our precise intelligent control? No. Who is able to control those?

13

THAT OLD COMPETITIVE EDGE

Competition. It can stimulate innovation when invention is needed. It can bring out the best efforts, for example, in athletic events or in other areas of endeavor. It can also be a trap (how many of us have been caught up in the question: who gets to walk off with the prize?)

"He who exalts himself shall be humbled." Much of my life seems to be living proof of that. Always trying to outperform this or that one, trying to establish something. Even when we sense that we're batting our heads against a wall, we continue.

There is a time and place for persistence. In a clear struggle of good-*vs*-evil there's no question that perseverance is vital. That's all the more reason why our motives need to be clear; we tend to rationalize sometimes. We might attribute a noble purpose to our efforts when our real goal is more self-seeking. In "win-win" scenarios that might not be too serious but, if a victory for us can risk a loss for someone else, this calls for some soul-searching. Rather than an insistence on winning, that might be a time for an attitude of "I must decrease." If so, we really need to accept that.

Accepting loss might make us look like losers in the eyes of people we wanted to impress. Take the hit. A jolt to the ego is far more perishable, and far less important, than the eventual inner serenity.

14

WHAT ABOUT US INCOMPETENTS ?

"*The effectual fervent prayer of a righteous man availeth much.*" Undoubtedly true; that's been shown in many ways. It is worth examining three conditions in that statement: *effectual, fervent,* and *righteous.* Sometimes it seems I've been told that great athletes win a lot of athletic contests. Hey, what about hacks like myself? Back to the subject here, what about distracted prayer of a half-baked Christian who is trying, belatedly and with difficulty, to learn how to become something better than half-baked – all the while counting a large and constantly growing accumulation of spiritual failures?

Every once in a while, at seemingly random times, I hear a really helpful statement in a Sunday sermon. Here's one: "*We really don't measure up but that's not the point.*" The explanation continued with the assurance – your Creator knows all about your limitations; He made you that way. Far better to face up to those limitations than to develop a big head (remember the parable about the Pharisee and the publican).

That *doesn't* mean that half-baked is good enough or that being fervent etc. is an unnecessary luxury. It just means that we don't start at the top; as with everything else, beginners have to acquire skill – and that takes time + practice. In the meantime, humility will carry you far as long as you don't ever lose your sincerity.

Don't ever lose your willingness to try, either. An old story from a source I can't recall depicts demons swapping all kinds of trouble-making ingredients that were enclosed in vials. One highly valued vial was very closely guarded; the devil was unwilling to share any of its contents. Naturally that prompted the question, "What's in there?" That vial contained discouragement.

LANGUAGE BARRIER?

What image comes to mind when we consider those, aside from preachers and other religious clergy, who profess a strong faith in God – those who express strong confidence in prayer? For much of my life, I must confess, individuals like that seemed to fall into one restrictive category or another. In this country it is fairly common, for example, to associate that characteristic with women and children – or exclusively with intellectuals – or with misfits, weaklings, fanatics, etc. That perception has been supported, unfortunately, by actions of some of the preachers, priests, and others who are supposedly leading the way. The perception is further encouraged by the entertainment industry's influence on today's popular "cultural" climate. What's good is labeled as bad and vice-versa. God is supposedly nonexistent or dead or irrelevant or preoccupied or uncaring or ⋯ (anything else He actually isn't). That's old news, of course, but prevailing attitudes warrant highlighting something we generally overlook: Almost the whole world can be taken by surprise and instantly learn how wrong the accepted wisdom has been. Often the reason why that comes as a surprise is that the world ignored the symptoms.

Ignoring symptoms comes from insensitivity to warnings. That's carelessness. Ignoring the calamity itself is more than careless; that's reckless. It has been clearly demonstrated that the dawn of this third millennium is a time much in need of reform. That reform won't be realized without another realization: Recognition and acceptance of Divine Will is essential. Survival as we know it depends on that. To understand it, you don't have to be "square" — "unhip" — etc., etc. You don't have to use unfamiliar words either, like "thee and thou and thy" — so what if the words have changed (how could words *not* have changed after all this time)? It's the ideas that matter; put those ideas in whatever words make sense to you.

Somewhere along the way it became popular to sideline the important ideas, branding all believers as weak or defenseless or some kind of misfit. Let's end that hoax once and for all.

Practical-minded people from all walks of life have seen through the false prophets. Unfortunately the sheer number of abuses (and abusers) create the mistaken impression that just about every expression of faith came with some ulterior motive. A reminder: never in history has there been any shortage of misinformation to obscure the truth; there's no substitute for vigilance.

Some of us have "a foot in both camps" — we're believers *and* we speak practical language. It's our task, somehow, to undo harm that the abusers have done. We need to reach the practical-minded skeptics, by straightforward appeals to reason in plain language that they understand — without "holier-than-thou" attitudes or any other angles. The task promises to be difficult. Difficult is not the same as impossible.

ANSWERS to PRAYERS: ANY HINTS?

1) We are encouraged to ask for desired outcomes.

2) Admit that our preferences, no matter how strongly felt, are guesses.

3) Include one overriding preference: conformance to the Divine will.

4) Add no unalterable preconditions of our own.

5) For any condition that really seems unalterable, item #3 covers it.

6) Work to help the desired outcome, but trying to force it might backfire.

7) We don't know exactly where to draw the line between helping and forcing.

8) Be understanding of side effects that others may care about.

9) We don't know when the answer will come.

10) Don't try to force the timing; it might interfere with the outcome.

11) Never believe that God is ignoring you; Infinite power = unlimited ability to do all.

12) Never believe that God is too busy; unlimited ability means that it's easy.

13) Never believe that God is uncaring (*Mt 10:30* - "every hair of your head ··· ").

14) Make enough room in your mind for surprises (desirable and undesirable).

15) Often the answers come in the form of events.

16) Accept the outcome, at least for the present moment.

17) If outcomes appear unsatisfactory, go back to step #1 and repeat.

18) Try to learn from whatever happens.

19) This list is very incomplete. So is any creature-generated list on this topic, probably.

ERRATA

There are always a few things noticed *after* the printing is done — *e.g.*, an extraneous "*of*" near mid-paragraph *1* on *p.* 39. Also, *pp.* 18-19 would be clearer in modified form shown here.

ANSWERS to PRAYERS: ANY HINTS?

1) We are encouraged to ask for desired outcomes.
2) Admit that our preferences, no matter how strongly felt, are guesses.
3) Include one overriding preference: conformance to the Divine will.
4) Add no unalterable preconditions of our own.
5) For any condition that really seems unalterable, item #3 covers it.
6) Work to help the desired outcome, but trying to force it might backfire.
7) We don't know exactly where to draw the line between helping and forcing.
8) Be understanding of side effects that others may care about.
9) We don't know when the answer will come.
10) Don't try to force the timing; it might interfere with the outcome.
11) Never believe that God is ignoring you; Infinite power = unlimited ability to do all.
12) Never believe that God is too busy; unlimited ability means that it's easy.
13) Never believe that God is uncaring (*Mt 10:30* - "every hair of your head … ").
14) Make enough room in your mind for surprises (desirable and undesirable).
15) Often the answers come in the form of events.
16) Accept the outcome, at least for the present moment.
17) If outcomes appear unsatisfactory, go back to step #1 and repeat.
18) Try to learn from whatever happens.
19) This list is very incomplete. So is any creature-generated list on this topic, probably.
20) Don't overlook the 17th line of the next page.

TIRED OF PRAYING OVER and OVER for the SAME THING?

not yet   *not yet*   *not yet*   *not yet*   *not yet*   *not yet*   *not yet*
not yet   *not yet*   *not yet*   *not yet*   *not yet*   *not yet*   *not yet*
not yet   *not yet*   *not yet*   *not yet*   *not yet*   *not yet*   *not yet*
not yet   *not yet*   *not yet*   *not yet*   *not yet*   *not yet*   *not yet*
not yet   *not yet*   *not yet*   *not yet*   *not yet*   *not yet*   *not yet*
not yet   *not yet*   *not yet*   *not yet*   *not yet*   *not yet*   *not yet*
not yet   *not yet*   *not yet*   *not yet*   *not yet*   *not yet*   *not yet*
not yet   *not yet*   *not yet*   *not yet*   *not yet*   *not yet*   *not yet*
not yet   *not yet*   *not yet*   *not yet*   *not yet*   *not yet*   *not yet*
not yet   *not yet*   *not yet*   *not yet*   *not yet*   *not yet*   *not yet*
not yet   *not yet*   *not yet*   *not yet*   *not yet*   *not yet*   *not yet*
not yet   *not yet*   *not yet*   *not yet*   *not yet*   *not yet*   *not yet*
not yet   *not yet*   *not yet*   *not yet*   *not yet*   *not yet*   *not yet*
not yet   *not yet*   *not yet*   *not yet*   *not yet*   *not yet*   *not yet*
not yet   *not yet*   *not yet*   *not yet*   *not yet*   *not yet*   *not yet*
not yet   *not yet*   *not yet*   *not yet*   *not yet*   *not yet*   *not yet*
not yet   *not yet*   *now yes*   *not yet*   *not yet*   *not yet*   *not yet*
not yet   *not yet*   *not yet*   *not yet*   *not yet*   *not yet*   *not yet*
not yet   *not yet*   *not yet*   *not yet*   *not yet*   *not yet*   *not yet*
not yet   *not yet*   *not yet*   *not yet*   *not yet*   *not yet*   *not yet*
not yet   *not yet*   *not yet*   *not yet*   *not yet*   *not yet*   *not yet*
not yet   *not yet*   *not yet*   *not yet*   *not yet*   *not yet*   *not yet*
not yet   *not yet*   *not yet*   *not yet*   *not yet*   *not yet*   *not yet*
not yet   *not yet*   *not yet*   *not yet*   *not yet*   *not yet*   *not yet*
not yet   *not yet*   *not yet*   *not yet*   *not yet*   *not yet*   *not yet*
not yet   *not yet*   *not yet*   *not yet*   *not yet*   *not yet*   *not yet*
not yet   *not yet*   *not yet*   *not yet*   *not yet*   *not yet*   *not yet*
not yet   *not yet*   ...

Be alert!

TIRED OF PRAYING OVER and OVER for the SAME THING?

no no no no no no no no no no no no no no no no no no
no no no no no no no no no no no no no no no no no no
no no no no no no no no no no no no no no no no no no
no no no no no no no no no no no no no no no no no no
no no no no no no no no no no no no no no no no no no
no no no no no no no no no no no no no no no no no no
no no no no no no no no no no no no no no no no no no
no no no no no no no no no no no no no no no no no no
no no no no no no no no no no no no no no no no no no
no no no no no no no no no no no no no no no no no no
no no no no no no no no no no no no no no no no no no
no no no no no no no no no no no no no no no no no no
no no no no no no no no no no no no no no no no no no
no no no no no no no no no no no no no no no no no no
no no no no no no no no no no no no no no no no no no
no no no no no no no no no no no no no no no no no no
no no no yes no no no no no no no no no no no no no no
no no no no no no no no no no no no no no no no no no
no no no no no no no no no no no no no no no no no no
no no no no no no no no no no no no no no no no no no
no no no no no no no no no no no no no no no no no no
no no no no no no no no no no no no no no no no no no
no no no no no no no no no no no no no no no no no no
no no no no no no no no no no no no no no no no no no
no no no no no no no no no no no no no no no no no no
no no no no no no no no no no no no no no no no no no
no no no no no no no no no no no no no no no no no no
no no no no no no no no no no no no no no no no no no
no no no no no no no no no no no no no no no no no no ···

Be alert!

19

MORE ABOUT ANSWERS: ANY CLUES?

When our lives don't resemble our wishes, the explanation could vary over a wide range. Often the most fundamental issue involves a yes-or-no question: Is the change we want consistent with the Divine will?

When the answer to that question is negative, that isn't always the worst news. It may be that another outcome we haven't thought of, with even better implications for us, is on the way. That's one case we could usually accept. The alternative, which we often try not to hear too clearly, is that the Christian way is the Way of the Cross; this earth isn't really home after all (as in a song from *Les Miserables*: " ⋯ but there are dreams that cannot be, and there are storms we cannot weather"). Even when that answer applies it's extremely important to realize that we haven't been abandoned. Keep an open mind for alternatives.

Frequently though, the answer to the fundamental question is unknown and/or either positive or conditional. It may be that more time is needed; just wait. It may be that we are complicating our own solution. Again there are contrasting possibilities ("Am I trying too hard to control a situation? Or too little? How can I tell where that line is?" Hmmm).

When the outcome is conditional, could a flaw in my character be complicating or delaying my answer? If we expect the most generous possible outcome *given all underlying conditions which we've been allowed to influence* that possibility can't be overlooked.

With no formula to cover every potential variation, it's crucial to stay in contact with the Source. The way to stay tuned is with quiet time and Scripture reading. Most of what's needed (*e.g.*, 99%) is provided for us.

Our cooperation and consent can provide the other 1%. Without obstructing free will God could dispense information we seek, influencing our decisions and aiming them in the right direction. For those unwilling to stay tuned I can't confidently offer much advice.

One clue from Scripture (*Pr 14:12* and *16:25*) describes a way that seems right but leads to destruction: this could explain why some of us must go through a period wherein so much seems to make no sense. We get so used to our own logic that, in order to learn not to lean on our own understanding (*Pr 3:5*), it has to fail us dramatically or spectacularly. Otherwise we could continue on our own logic, in effect unguided. One possible outcome would be a false sense of security, due to unawareness of flaws deeply ingrained in our old style of self-direction. If that happens over extended period, no wonder that distortions occur during the correction interval. It's time to "revise the template" – stop trying to fit every event into the pattern we've mentally constructed and held for so long ("*Think not of things of old ⋯ *").

It's worthwhile to consider this hypothetical scenario: For some outcome of very special interest to you, suppose you were given a choice between two alternatives –
  · complete and absolute power for you to control the outcome, regardless of whether your choice conforms to God's wishes
  · an opportunity to receive, at an unforeseen time under unforeseeable conditions, an outcome chosen by God.
You would be ahead with the second choice. Lucky you – that's what you have anyway.

21

James L. Farrell

HE'S TRANSITIONED OVER

*Following is a brief eulogy I gave at the
funeral of my brother, Bob Farrell. He
was a great guy, and he is now where
great guys go.*

Bob's childhood began just three years before mine,
so my recollections will cover most of the time
intended. In the beginning about all I can remember
is playing with toy trucks in the bed and singing songs
in the back yard. There was an awareness, though,
that I had friends; there were sisters and there was a
guy named Bud (that's what we called him in those
days).

Somewhere toward the end of those toddler days the
family moved to a different neighborhood - first on
Campbell Ave and shortly after about a block away, to
Leland Ave. 2535 Leland Ave. Emerging out from the
fog of toddlerhood I was becoming more aware of the
world around - and noticing how some of the things
that were happening were making life complicated.
One of those things was the way our Dad had to go
out of town for work. When your place of work has no
contract in the city where you live, you go where the
work is. There was a stint in Wisconsin, another one
in Knoxville (Tennessee), and another one in Pittsburgh
(Pennsylvania) – for months at a time. Another
complication was underworld interference in labor
unions. We've read about those things in more
modern times. Well, in Chicago of the 1940s, it
affected the building trades. Underworld figures were
attending union meetings, trying to drive decisions in
the wrong direction. Our Dad resisted those efforts.

22

Learning Robert's Rules of Order, at one point he appealed the decision of the chair.

That was a dangerous thing to do. One night, parked outside the house at 2535 Leland with lights out, there was a car full of thugs waiting for our Dad to come home. What did Bob do? He went out the back door, down the alley, a few blocks further to where our Dad was – and told him about the danger. That prevented what otherwise would have been a disaster. Bob wasn't yet a teenager at that time, but he set in motion a trait that would carry forward through his entire life: he was a vital figure to have around when a rescue was needed.

A third factor that was complicating life was the landlord at 2535 Leland. He didn't like kids (at least other people's kids) – and there were five of us. Eviction wasn't a legal option but, when he sold the place, the new owner had the legal right to force us to move away. Although our Dad earned enough to pay rent, there was a housing shortage in Chicago at that time. No place to be found. For a few months all seven of us (parents + 5 kids) lived with an aunt. Being only ten at the time, I was somewhat oblivious to the hardship (a hard-working Dad and a Mother doing everything possible to keep it all together, buckling under pressure from sources beyond control). To me at the time, the new neighborhood meant a different bunch of guys to play baseball and softball with. That's how almost all my free time was spent.

From my viewpoint during those years, it was a tremendous help to have an older brother. Seeing everything for the first time, I found this world to be a very confusing place. It was great to have a brother who would explain the things that were important at the time. Friends, jokes, songs. How to get along with girls. How to tease girls (to learn that, you start by teasing your sisters – and I'm afraid we did more than our share of that; to their everlasting credit, they didn't hold it against us). How to play softball or baseball in spring and summer, football in the autumn and winter. Wherever there was a vacant lot, that was our diamond. For football in the autumn and winter all we needed was a street. The curbs on each side were the sidelines and, for goal lines, there were trees and lamp-posts. Bob was the gifted athlete. I was always a below-average athlete (still am and always will be), but I was always included in the games – because I was his brother.

Soon a place became available – we couldn't call it a house (a dwelling above a store front that was first a grocery store, then a saloon, then a laundromat). During a housing shortage you take it. We lived at 3601 N. Ashland. Another new bunch of guys for softball or baseball in the vacant lots and football in the streets (again from my limited perspective). We were there for three years before the family moved to Rockford Ill. By that time Bob was a high-school senior (yes, he played varsity baseball that year). No longer a child, and not much longer an adolescent – shortly after graduation, he became Marine Corporal Robert J. Farrell, battle-tested combat veteran. His modesty wouldn't let him talk about it much but, more than once, he was decorated for that.

During that time another life-long trait surfaced: courage and humor in the presence of adversity. That trait was obvious even to those who didn't know him for a long time, and hadn't seen him on many occasions. One of those persons is my wife, Cruz Maria. She really wanted to be here. Couldn't make it happen. She said, "he was a great man" – and she meant it. Another is my son, Mike. Although a computer science freshman (not a writer), on Friday he wanted to write something; this is what he came up with: "Your laughing spirit flows eternal from the skies."

During Bob's time in the Marine Corps, one writer who was becoming more famous was the old sportswriter, Damon Runyan. He wrote many things (one of his short stories became the basis for a successful Broadway musical, "Guys and Dolls") – but I want now to draw attention to one of his statements to the effect that

We'll all meet again some day in the "tavern at the end of the road"

I'd like all of us to take comfort from that thought because, for us at this time, it means that we aren't saying good-bye. We're saying good-night, Bob; we will meet again at the end of the road. In the meantime, we want to say thanks to you, for making us laugh so hard so often. Above all, we want to express our profound gratitude to God for leading you to the *HEAVEN* at the end of the road.

FAVORITE SCRIPTURAL PASSAGES
(not verbatim)

Sometimes a passage from scripture can strike a resonant chord. Here are some gems:

What is impossible to man is possible with God.

I will set your foot upon a rock.

I will give you words that cannot be refuted and wisdom to communicate them.

The stone that the builders rejected became the cornerstone.

Trust God with all your heart, and lean not to your own understanding.

In all your ways acknowledge Him and He will guide your paths.

For I know the plans I have for you; plans of peace and not affliction ⋯

I have known you from eternity.

The Lord will finish what He has started in me.

Think not of things of old. See I do a new thing - do you not perceive it?

26

I will find a way in the wilderness; rivers in the desert.

Treasures in secret hiding places

Call to me and I will hear ...I will show you great things ...which you know not.

Delight in the ways of the Lord and He will give you the desires of your heart.

No good thing shall be denied him who does the will of the Lord.

Ask and you shall receive, seek and you shall find, knock and it shall be opened···
NOTE: this doesn't say *when.*

Even though you say you see Him not, the case is before Him.

Wait, I say, wait on the Lord.

James L. Farrell

KEEP THOSE LACES TIED WHILE YOU'RE
on the BENCH

Those of us who are "hacks" at sports — natural-born mediocre (or less) athletes — often have a history of playing in high school but, for anything organized, not beyond. Even those limited experiences are less than stellar. Taken out of the sports realm, though, they can offer lessons bigger than the outcome of a game.

During spring season my high school friends became quite accustomed to my incessant claim: *if the coach only recognized my capability, I'd be on the playing field instead of on the bench all the time.* One entire season passed that way and, after another season was nearly over, I no longer bothered to tie the laces of my spike shoes. Late in one of the last games, after our left fielder was injured, my ears rang with the words *"Farrell get out there into left field."* No time to tie the laces. The first ball pitched to the next batter produced a high fly to left field. To complicate matters, the sun had never seemed brighter than at that time on that day.

Have you ever tried to walk, let alone run, while wearing baseball spikes untied? It seems as if there could be enough string to wind around your leg a few hundred times and still have enough left to tie every knot known to all boy scouts and all sailors combined.

Not only did I fail to catch the fly ball; I fell down chasing it. After vainly throwing the retrieved ball into the infield — much too late — I could see my friends literally rolling in the grass laughing at me. It's funny now but it wasn't funny then.

More important than funny is application of this lesson to life: Keep those laces tied while you're on the bench.

28

BOX SCORE

inning →	1	2	3	4	5	6	7	8	9	
Pessimism	99	99	99	99	99	99	99	99	99	L
Optimism	0	0	0	0	0	0	0	0	1	W

<u>Play-by-play</u> With two out in the ninth, Optimism hit a solo home run to WIN THE GAME.

Example: Consider the guy whose haphazard relationships with hundreds of girls, over a period of years, never amounted to much of anything lasting. The combination of experiences left him more bewildered than satisfied. Mundane reminders seemed to come from everywhere, even seeing leftover rice on the sidewalk outside Church (yeah, guys get that way too). Then one day a woman he loved fell in love with him; they married. The past didn't hurt him. In fact, it helped him to appreciate his success.

Example: Consider the guy who was sick for years. Then one day he was cured. The past didn't make him sick any more. In fact, it helped him to appreciate his health.

Not every problem accumulates a score that has to be undone.

James L. Farrell

SPOTLIGHT on the GOOD GUYS
(for a CHANGE)

Hardly a day goes by now without mention somewhere of a priest who committed a crime against children. Outrageous – no question about it. No question in my mind either that all of them should have been instantly exposed and put beyond reach of potential victims. Since that wasn't done, anyone who shielded them should now be fired (not playing God here; zero tolerance). That's not at all too harsh; I said fired, not lynched. Since that wasn't done, I frankly question the judgment – and competence – of the whole hierarchy. My denomination lost an giant amount of credibility in the Christian community. How many centuries it would take to regain that is anyone's guess.

So here we are with two groups having things in common (*e.g.*, all priests wear the same Roman collar) but one thing that's very different (a small subgroup within who are as guilty as sin). It's always hard to understand when the culprits – in this case the deviates and also their protectors who covered up for them – are supposedly in the business of leading us to God. Shouldn't they be immune to blunders that undermine this higher purpose? Every decade we relearn – by examples from all directions – they're not immune. The same faults that plague other institutions affect churches too. Wherever there's management you may find Dilbert's boss.

What's to be done about the others – who didn't commit any crimes? We might begin by remembering that those are really the large majority. We are constantly being told to avoid stereotyping. Most Arabs don't fly planes into buildings. Most Jews aren't filthy-rich business owners. Most Germans aren't mad scientists and most Irish aren't hopeless alcoholics (I'm half Irish and half German). Most blacks aren't filthy-rich basketballers. The list goes on, but you get the point. Generalizations are out.

Generalizations are clearly wrong for the lucky majority like myself, taught by nuns in grade school and priests throughout high school (Augustinians) plus undergraduate college (Jesuits). The thought of any one of those dedicated teachers doing anything so off-the-wall is unthinkable. Absolutely no comparison between them and the degenerates.

The Catholic church is especially vulnerable here due to past assertions of superiority, alienating other Christian denominations. Megatons of ammunition have been donated to those wanting reasons to quit and/or hate Catholicism (or even all of Christianity). Motivations aside, only a step-by-step path is available to the rest of us. We can't make the disgrace vanish but we can leave the culprits to their court-decreed fate and inch ahead without them (that's not overkill either – God ultimately controls the penalties and manages the forgiveness department, while giving creatures the grave and inescapable responsibility to protect innocent children). Christ never envisioned a Church free of attack, even from within. He did say, though, that the attackers would not prevail. Inquisition didn't finish it; neither will this (by the way, the level of gravity isn't that far different). A reminder: sacrifices by the vast majority have not been in vain.

The same applies in the prisoner abuse scandal; again a degraded environment spawns monstrous deeds. Next millennium, as this planet's history relates crimes against children and prisoners, it will remain true: guilt rests on a small fraction from each community.

JOURNEY THROUGH the UNKNOWN

In selecting a trajectory for spacecraft, an issue that repeatedly arises is"optimization" – for example, a time-optimal path reaches a destination faster than any other; a fuel-optimal path reaches a destination with minimum energy expended. Those two aren't the same; a trajectory that is optimum (best) for one characteristic isn't best for another. Before a "best" choice can be made, then, it must be decided exactly what is meant by best. This could be least time, least fuel, or some compromise between (based on a specified relative value attached to speed and fuel economy). Alternatively, various other desirable features (of which there are many possibilities) could be taken into account. So the overall task includes identifying exactly what's best, and then finding the trajectory that is best from that standpoint.

Consider a spacecraft initially on a chosen path, but veering away afterwards. It is then possible to perform a new optimization starting from the deviated state. Overall mission success, though unable to match the original choice, will be the best achievable once the deviation occurs. The process can be repeated over and over, with each instance resulting in another "plan B" (and generally another sacrifice – *e.g.*,some facet of the mission becomes more difficult or may have to be omitted).

The analogy with decisions made during a lifetime can now be clarified. We will ignore unimportant choices (*e.g.*, selections from a restaurant menu) and acknowledge immediately that, at any crossroads, both the criterion (what's best) and the means to achieve it can often be unclear. Nevertheless some procedure exists that is superior to others. Can we get to it somehow?

A Christian answer to the question is clear from *Rom 8:28* (⋯ all things work together to those ⋯ called to His purpose ⋯). When described within the context of a guidance strategy, certain aspects seem to stand out:

* Knowledge. Only God can figure out all this, in the presence of forces we can't even understand let alone control.
* Power. Only God can take all that information and set the scene enabling us to succeed if we cooperate.
* Generosity. Only God would bestow all those favors.
* Patience. If we sidestep what's best, we're offered second best. If we sidestep what's second best, we're offered the next best choice ⋯ If there are more setbacks than Apollo 13, we're offered whatever partial rescue remains available.

The view from this perspective should trigger a grateful response from us all.

DID the ENVY JUST DISAPPEAR?

A prominent syndicated columnist defines the set of American male adults as a bunch of failed baseball players. A confession: as a kid in grade school I dreamed about becoming a major league baseball player – not just any major leaguer but (of course) the best ever in the history of the game. Naturally, since all things were possible at that age, I had additional visions of becoming a famous football player plus a great singer plus ⋯ hey, since the sky was the limit, throw in a few dozen more pipe dreams.

Now the weekly news magazines, beyond pages describing all the terrible national and international happenings, print an occasional book review or interview about some celebrity who actually realized some of those ambitions. After seeing both of those in *Newsweek* today I searched my mind for the jealousy that seemed so reasonable to expect – but it didn't come. Whet happened? Is it the perception, finally, that fame and fortune really "ain't where it's at" after all? Is it a recognition of the enormous burdens that often accompany the dubious privilege of having a big name?

The explanation isn't due to any loss of interest in what prompted those pipe dreams in the first place. Clearly it can't be due to comparable successes in my own life either. Did the first paragraph mention sports? I couldn't make first string in high school and, beyond that, not much happened other than intramural company teams or pickup games. Was show-biz mentioned? Anything I've experienced in performing has been strictly local – many tiers below what's described in celebrity interviews and book reviews. Love life? A bumpy ride if there ever was one.

Still the games were fun, the songs were great, and the dates made an active social life (it costs me nothing to hope that every one of them found the right husband and lived happily ever after). Best of all, it isn't over. Sports: a guy can still play tennis (even with all those mistakes). Music: there still are repeated opportunities to put a song across. Love: I still love my wife. That's not just to be chivalrous; she's been worth the wait − and I waited a lifetime to find her.

There are countless other blessings. Sibling, son, daughter, friend. Work (not at all a burden; it stays interesting). Also it keeps the wheels turning − and the bills paid. Etc. etc. etc.; no good thing has been denied.

Make your own list; everyone has a different combination to recall. It doesn't have to be glamorous or dramatic. More important is a grateful attitude, fueled by a willingness to recognize clearly and unmistakably the Source of all these gifts.

Now as if to remove the punch from that "downgrading of celebrities" − the same issue of *Newsweek* showed, just before the last page, another famous one who actually puts much effort into charitable causes. He notes, in his words, how wrong is the idea that "the prosperous few can live separate from the poverty of the many." If he can succeed in changing some of that − OK, *there's* something worthy of our envy. Point noted.

NARROW PATHS

We are all familiar with "rules of the road" that restrict our driving; we aren't allowed to go whenever and wherever we want. Whether we realize it or not, restrictions are also applied on the water – there are shipping lanes, for example. Historically, though, there were ships before there were laws. That partially explains why it happens, more often than you might expect, that a rogue ship breaks all rules and potentially endangers whatever may be in its present or future path.

Fortunately, there were laws before there were aircraft. That partially explains why it happens far *less* often that pilots act independent of air traffic control – and when they do, they promptly become *former* pilots. Otherwise imagine the chaos and the danger in the vicinity of a busy airport. It doesn't require expertise in aircraft operations to realize this: When there are large numbers of objects moving fast within a limited space, many of the possible interactions are decidedly unfavorable.

The statement just observed applies to real live persons as well. If you don't know the right way, try to find it. If you do know the right way, follow it; don't veer to the right nor the left. Don't go where you clearly don't belong (you might promptly become a *former* real live person). Not that every decision has life-or-death consequences, but all have ramifications (often including unknown ones) that call for our best effort. It seems worth recalling here, too, that seemingly minor decisions can sometimes have bigger-than-expected effects.

FRAMED

"Exercise caution in your business affairs; for the world is full of trickery" - Desiderata (Child of the Universe) Max Ehrmann, 1927; Copyright: Robt. Bell, Melrose, MA

Once upon a time there lived a manorlord, in a wealthy estate whose beautiful landscape was threatened by a failing sprinkler system. Whereupon he summoned the gardener and instructed him to replace the valve. "Nay sire, "the gardener replied, "I have discovered a thirty-inch gash in the hose, whereas the valve has faithfully performed its function throughout." But the lord of the manor insisted, "The valve shall be replaced; I have chosen a provider for this item, which must be substituted for the original even as the defective hose segment is repaired." So forthwith the two changes were effected concurrently. And thus it was, from that day forward, that the manorlord could say, "The sprinkler works fine - ever since we had that valve replaced."

Imagine this scenario transported to the world of high-tech, wherein complex systems work successfully if and only if every constituent is correct. From the input to the final output there may be many stages, not all of equal complexity. The most complicated subsystem is a source of worry to managers who can't take time to understand much about the technical operation. If the techie in charge of that main complication is irreverent to managers, he can be a constant target as long as there's a problem *anywhere* between starting input and final output. Another worker can then displace him as the local expert in one area from that day forward.

37

Something comparable to the "valve/hose" situation happened to this writer several years ago. Enough time has since passed to allow what seemed impossible then: an even-tempered assessment of the overall results. What seemed most important at the time wasn't really paramount (the words "local" and "one" in the last sentence of the preceding paragraph are significant). Another worker capitalizing on that kind of opportunity doesn't really make him indistinguishable from Dorian Gray – and the biggest loser was the corporation itself (subsequent events outside of it gained me more than the lost status within it). Lessons learned are fairly obvious. Don't take an inflexible position; not everyone observes the old advice from a former U.S. President (Calvin Coolidge: "If it ain't broke don't fix it"). Don't confuse knowledge with authority; you can be right and still lose – but if that happens you can win back much more elsewhere later. (This narrative also contains some fairly obvious lessons for corporate managers as well, but that isn't the focus here.)

To illustrate further how we sometimes overestimate severity of an event, imagine stretching this example into unfamiliar – far more forbidding – territory. Law-enforcement experts often point out that suspects have been convicted of crimes they didn't commit. How do they ever contain their rage?

NOT a QUITTER

Most of us have been there at one time or another. This writer is no exception. It can grow within a short period or build up over years. It can happen within the walls of a corporation or a home, or in various other places. Every statement is twisted, resented, misconstrued, interrupted, contradicted, and demolished in a hundred of other ways. Without communication nothing gets resolved but communication lines are cut. Because stakes are high we tried desperately. Tried it all but nothing works. Now what?

We have no limitless formulas here but there are some unfailing truths:

The decision to surrender every detail of control to God is a key step. Initially it is often brought on by unhappiness. All we can generate at first is consent, not joyful willingness. After some months, we finally begin – but only begin – to be comfortable with it. That decision solves one problem, though: Everything that happens after it is just what is supposed to happen. Unless I'm trying to override the controls, they're being driven by all-powerful, all-wise, and infinitely generous hands. Programmed by the only real expert Programmer. Care to improve on that? Not a good idea to try.

Faith isn't identical to confidence that a specific request *will* be granted, but certainty that God has power and the generosity to grant it. The request might well be granted if consistent with the overall plan, or denied if not. Either way, in the long term, the deck is stacked in our favor. The outcome may be contingent on our cooperation; we might enable (not force) our goal by supporting a vital circumstance.

Be realistic in evaluating apparent situations (improvement or the lack thereof), but recognize that they're only apparent. Don't rule out the possibility that circumstances are more favorable than evident. Keep bridges intact and stay alert (without overanalyzing) while waiting. Another key clue: keep waiting – without complaint.

Believe that partial credit is given for imperfect effort. A little effort from us can be enough to trigger a *big* assist from God.

Adrian Rogers' tapes on *Ps 23*: No valley without a mountain. Similarly, I once heard these thoughts in a Sunday sermon: When nothing seems to make sense, when genuine effort is made to solve an important and urgent problem, and all those efforts end in seemingly endless repetitious frustration and confusion, admit that we don't control our circumstances. Control is in the hands of an infinitely wise and loving Supreme Being who deserves our complete trust and patience. Persevere. *Never* give up hope. I once attributed this kind of logic to some abstract theological brainwashing. *Wrong*!! The Good Shepherd wouldn't lead you through a valley just to leave you stranded there.

BEFORE and AFTER STORIES

STORY #1: THE BUS STOPS HERE

BEFORE

The year was 1993. My daughter and my son, then 13 and 9 years old (respectively), had left home with their runaway mother. Given the choice at that age, children are more likely to select the stay-at-home mom than the go-to-work dad. Still, all the defense mechanisms – that work like a champ against a runaway – could never make the kids' absence OK. The school bus stopping outside was a reminder: the door wasn't about to open with a burst of energy from exuberant kids eager to start their play activities. Not any more – and no way to rationalize an explanation for that loss. Inescapable reality: "shared custody" only *sounds* balanced; it isn't.

AFTER

Year 2002. A recent visit with my daughter and her new husband was a fun time. My son, attending the local community college, is back home. Although my work has made it necessary for me to be programming for years (actually decades), every year brings out more new software than I can track. Guess who is providing help that turns out to be absolutely crucial: that young son in the local community college. The things I'm learning from him would have taken me forever to find on my own. What a deal.

STORY #2: in the *CEREAL*?

BEFORE
It was late 1995. After a life-changing event, it takes some time to figure out where you are going. During that interim, confusion and discouragement are no strangers. On one memorable morning, breakfast (alone, as was now customary) was followed by an exceptionally dejected frame of mind. It seemed that nothing was working. Normally during any prayer I don't dare hint at anything that even remotely resembles a complaint. That day, though, the thought crossed my mind about a Scriptural passage to the effect that you won't be given a snake if you ask for a fish; you won't be given a stone if you ask for bread. You've heard of the expression "crying in his beer" – well, I felt like crying in my cereal practically. Almost two years earlier I had already made up my mind, that God owns my life – all of it. Still, my thoughts and feelings couldn't be escaped (*"You said I wouldn't be given a stone if I asked for bread ⋯ "*). Lost with no clear way to navigate out of the maze.

AFTER
It must really be true that, with the right background preparation, prayers uttered in sadness will be heard. I was about to experience a clear demonstration of generosity from Heaven. Not long after that morning, an almost impossible set of circumstances (beginning with a "problem" – a flight that was more than two hours late) steered me toward the woman who is truly the love of my life. We married within a year. The accompanying photos were taken on August 10, 1996.

EVENTS in MOTION

Occasionally a decision is thrust into our hands with unexpected ramifications. The decade was the 1980s, before the end of apartheid rule in South Africa. I had been teaching navigation seminars, in cooperation with people who regularly submitted a "shopping list" of courses to various potential sponsors. Among the prospects was an organization (government, industry, or something in between) from South Africa, interested only in one – mine. The usual arrangements were made, this time including items involved with international travel. A cascade of events seemed to be sliding toward completion.

Something didn't feel quite right. It wasn't that some groups advocated complete boycott of everything related to that country; there were informed voices within South Africa opposing the boycotts for their unintended consequences (hardship inflicted on the poor). Still, any possibility of becoming an accomplice to injustice was unsettling; I was becoming uncharacteristically depressed. Finally a tennis partner (another sports hack) made a useful suggestion to me: Submit to the client the following question: Will material from this course be used to conduct any operations helpful for maintaining apartheid?

To their everlasting credit, those managing the seminars presented the question in just that form. Since the answer received was defensive and evasive, the plan was scrapped with no further pressure on me. This happened the day before those involved were scheduled to pick up passports. The seminar managers willingly accepted the loss, including whatever additional lost opportunities might have resulted from that time forward. Unfortunate as that may be, the alternative would have been a far greater problem.

When something is nagging at your brain, it can be just the result of unnecessary worrying. Be alert, though; it might mean that events are carrying you into a situation where you don't belong.

THIS IS SUPPOSED to BE a REHEARSAL?

The problem wasn't the lines. Those familiar with *The Music Man* realize that, although the number isn't simple — "*Trouble (right here in River City)*" — it can be learned well enough to be presented fluently. I had all the words, tempo, and moves committed to memory. Down cold. In the mind of the director, that was just the problem. Too predictable. Here was that very tough lady's reaction:

"You think that the people in this cast should listen to you just because you're the lead? *NO!* Now while you recite those words you've memorized I'm going to draw them away from you." Then as the music resumed she did just that. Toward the end of the number I had about a fourth of the cast left with me.

For her next move she ordered me to forget the script and expound on any other topic — as the cast members were urged to heckle, contradict, or tune me out. I failed that test completely and, in a repeated attempt at a later rehearsal, completely failed again. Her point: In real life you can't predict others' reactions; no one is following any script. So make this scene real or else it's fake (you're just going through the motions).

On a third attempt at this grueling exercise I chose a topic that had bothered me for years: world hunger. As the usual heckling etc. began I was able to cut it off. "*No!*" I heard myself saying, while looking straight at each one in turn, *Not this time!*" That wasn't because I had all the facts; my feelings were a vital reason why I could silence criticism. When you feel

46

strongly about an issue your conviction is powerful enough to face down opposition. On this occasion by the time I was finished, a number of the cast members were crying. The director had taught a valuable lesson to all of us.

Thee is another irony in all this — how much reality there is in theatre *when it's done right*. That goes hand-in-hand with how much make-believe there is in the supposedly real world of big business. In any case, your convictions are important — and observable.

If our stated convictions are observable by other creatures, how much more are our beliefs (including our hidden thoughts) observable by the One Who *invented* creatures?

A LITTLE BOY from HAITI
[Anecdote from Church - Holy Trinity, Glen Burnie MD]

The following experience was recounted by Sr. Vivian Patnode, Religious of Jesus and Mary, from a time when she was substituting for a teacher during a lunch recess:

Each child's aluminum plate had been filled with rice and beans, topped with a splatter of vegetables. They gave thanks to God for this gift of food as all sat. Haitian children have the tradition of eating in silence and, when they finish, of going out into the yard to play. with sticks and small rocks.

For most of them it would be their one and only meal that day. Suddenly she noticed a seven-year-old boy pulling out his backpack. Not able to imagine what he would want to take out at that time, she said "Please eat first; then you can take out your book." As his eyes searched her face she heard a swishing sound, causing her to move closer to see what was happening. She asked, "What's in there that you want so badly?" Holding up an empty plastic bag, he looked her straight in the eye and begged, "please, Sr. Vivian, let me put the rest of my meal in the plastic bag for the rest of my family so everyone at home will have something to eat tonight." She later learned that this boy did that whenever the school offered him a meal.

Great minds (and much lesser ones like mine) have searched their brains trying to figure out how to end hunger, malnutrition, and starvation. We don't have that power. Even those at powerful positions in this most powerful nation have encountered opposition while trying to solve the problem. A U.S.-sponsored

48

<u>Food for Peace</u> program in the 1980s, with participation of civil servants genuinely trying to help, ran into resistance from powerful (or power-crazy) elements within the countries that could have received the benefit. Later there was the disastrous effort to intervene in Somalia.

Extreme discouragement, because it is so hard to help, doesn't remove the obligation to try other approaches. The stakes are too high to ignore. An individual can't do it all, but can do something, some little thing. Try to be alert for the next chance to help someone who needs something. With the right preparation you can find your individual assignment (which, as Scripture shows, has wide variation – one man is invited to accompany Jesus but declines; another asks to come along and is told instead to return to his people and tell them of his experience; others are instructed *not* to tell what He had done). Finding your niche doesn't need to be easy; it just needs to be done.

The greatest individual I ever met in person was the late Dr. Tom Dooley, missionary doctor and author (*The Night They Burned the Mountain* , *Deliver Us from Evil* , and *The edge of Tomorrow* were three of his books I read). He said that we have to be satisfied with small accomplishments. That seems to imply that he didn't recognize the vastness of his own accomplishments. Maybe something like that is, or will be, true of you; don't rule out the possibility. Sr. Vivian Patnode provides one example of someone who didn't stop trying.

James L. Farrell

NOT REALLY ALONE
[Anecdote from Church - Holy Trinity, Glen Burnie MD]

Generations ago when a brave from one Indian tribe reached a certain age (early teens), there was a rite of passage he had to undergo — he had to spend a night alone in the woods. The experience as recounted by one went something like this:

The evening began with apprehension, not surprisingly, at starting an encounter never before attempted. Also unsurprising was the way time seemed to pass so slowly. With increasing darkness came increasing sounds or increasing sensitivity to sounds — or both. The variety of sounds and the resulting visions conjured up by the imagination were likewise on the rise as the time continued its forward crawl. Although fatigue exerted a powerful influence, fear was stronger; who wants to sleep when an attack could suddenly emerge from any direction:?

At long length — seemingly after eons had passed — dawn started to break. Initially that brought another scare: Uh-oh, what's that shadow from back of that tree over there?

That shadow was his father, with a bow and arrow. He had been there all the time.

SMOOTHING OUT the HARD STUFF
[Anecdote from Church - Holy Trinity, Glen Burnie MD]
- obtained via internet]

A small congregation in the foothills of the Great Smokey Mountains built a new sanctuary on a piece of land willed to them by a church member. Ten days before the new church was to open, the local building inspector informed the pastor that the parking lot was inadequate for the size of the building. Until the church doubled the size of the parking lot, they would not be able to use the new sanctuary.

Unfortunately, the church with its undersized lot had used every inch of their land except for the mountain against which it had been built. In order to build more parking spaces, they would have to move the mountain out of the back yard.

Undaunted, the pastor announced the next Sunday morning that he would meet that evening with all members who had "mountain moving faith." They would hold a prayer session asking God to remove the mountain from the back yard and somehow provide enough money to have it paved and painted before the scheduled opening dedication service the following week.

At the appointed time, 24 of the congregation's 300 members assembled for prayer. They prayed for nearly three hours. At ten o'clock the pastor said the final "Amen." "We'll open next Sunday as scheduled," he assured everyone. "God has never let us down before, and I believe He will be faithful this time, too."

The next morning as he was working in his study there came a loud knock at his door. When he called "come in", a rough-looking construction foremen appeared, removing his hat as he entered.   "Excuse me, Reverend. I'm from Acme Construction Company over in the next county. We're building a huge shopping mall. We need some fill dirt. Would you be willing to sell us a chunk of that mountain behind the church? We'll pay you for the dirt we remove and pave all the exposed area free of charge, if we can have it right away. We can't do anything else until we get the dirt in and allow it to settle properly."

The little church was dedicated the next Sunday as originally planned and there were far more members with "mountain moving faith" on opening Sunday than there had been the previous week.

HARDENING the SOFT STUFF

[Anecdote from Church - St. Bernadette, Severn MD]

The new gardener always took special care to treat all plants gently. It seemed common sense; leaves, stems, and petals look fragile. You aren't exactly supposed to surround those things with something like a pipe wrench and close those jaws tight. OK, so that's an exaggeration but you get the idea. Obvious.

The old gardener wouldn't be bothered with such niceties. Need to move a plant from one location to another? Well, then, grab the thing unceremoniously by whatever was a suitable grasping site, and pull it up as fast as you like. Then plunk it down, just as fast, into its new place. End of operation.

Appalling, the young gardener thought. At what foundry or mechanic's garage did this bull-in-a-china-shop guy learn how to handle sensitive things?

Fast forward a few months. Whose plants were surviving and whose were failing? Surprise: the plants responded far better to the rough handling. Too much coddling somehow didn't work. Moral of the story: Want some things (or some people) to be robust? Then give them some adversity; nothing like a little preparation for what's destined to come.

NEVER MIND CHILDHOOD; DIDN'T the HURTS COME from the OPPOSITE SEX?

At the risk of inserting material that's out of place, this topic warrants attention just due to the vast number of people urgently looking for answers. I once gave a 2-hour seminar for those who place romantic disappointments high on the hurt-list. This assumes that we were not mistreated in childhood and haven't experienced severe injury, disabling illness, nor criminal attack. Still, absence of love carries ramifications; we are not merely acting like cry-babies when we ponder the cost — provided that we proceed beyond mere philosophizing and look at action-inducing answers. Issues under consideration included:
• One-way (not mutual) attraction; either direction but not both: why so often (hint: it's like random)
• Why repeated failures don't make you a loser (you may be counting, no one else is)
• A *restricted*-duration "sliding window" of recollection can limit accumulation of hurts
• Perspective for various psycho-theories: As an expert authority on your life you are second *only* to God.
• Life-giving info from scriptural passages.
• Would you be offended if the one(s) who betrayed you won the lottery? (Shouldn't care)
• Develop what you have and stay prepared for sudden unexpected opportunities.

The class addressed topics often deemphasized, without repeating material that is overemphasized elsewhere. Spiritual concepts were included, in the context of real-life encounters, without language sounding stilted to the layman. Sexual attraction was confronted with accent on the latter word (attraction) instead of the first word of that phrase — this is important for reasons that seem to escape recognition:

There is no universal standard of attractiveness. Why isn't that obvious? As one teacher said during college days — attraction is a relative thing; two hyenas probably look good to each other. To test that theory during my single days, I once risked asking a girl I was dating (who was far above me in the attractiveness department) why she wanted to date me instead of anyone else. Her answer: "I have irrational tastes." I never forgot that; you might want to retain it as well.

If you think that you're "unattractive" stop believing that. And stop trying to analyze what defies analysis. A brilliant mind from the past (Pascal) said that the heart has reasons that reason doesn't know ⋯ . If 99% of the members of the opposite sex prefer hundreds of others before you, so what? Your future partner will probably come from that other one percent — "par for the course" (except for those gifted few with a much higher percent; let's hope they don't lose focus due to all that attention). Among that one percent, you might be attracted to only a small fraction of those. Recognize that one percent of one percent translates to one in ten thousand — and even when it's mutual, there may be other circumstances in the way. No one ever guaranteed that this would be easy. Remember, though, how many days there are in a year — and often with multiple encounters in a day. How many times do you really need to succeed?

Commonly accepted practices such as excessive dependence on individual counseling were questioned. Not that counseling should be abolished, but it's probably overdone. An effort was made to increase attendees' confidence in their own inner resources. No shrink needed; go to the One who invented minds.

ENERGY FROM THOUGHTS - FACT
(What "psychic" *isn't*)

Now we'll consider the question of psychic energy. Before calling it good or bad, let me make a comparison with the signals that come into your TV antenna. Those signals are extremely weak. *How weak?* We're all familiar with light bulbs — 100 watt, 60 watt, ⋯ well, you'd be amazed at what a pitifully small fraction of a watt is captured by your TV antenna — even when your picture is good without cable. Why does it work with such a low-power signal? Well, when your picture is good, you can be sure that the interference is even weaker than the weak signal, and your TV set is sensitive as well as accurately tuned to the channel you select. That last statement actually implies more than just the right carrier frequency but, for our purposes here, let's just say that communication is good when the receiver is on the right wavelength. Even though that oversimplifies things, it can be used here as an expression - and here we can interpret that to mean all of the necessary conditions for successful reception.

The next thing to be said here will sound like a digression but it isn't. In the mid-80s three members of the Volunteers for Medical Engineering were offered the privilege of attending a course in Neurophysiology at the JHU school of medicine. I grabbed the chance and attended almost all the classes over a period of one semester — right in there with all those med students. One of the main topics covered was the way information is transmitted. Again only a rudimentary idea is enough for us right now; picture nerve endings, axons, ions (*i.e.*, atoms with missing electrons) — whatever works to conjure up in your mind the transfer of impulses, physiologically. Well, as soon as ions were brought into the picture, to me that meant some electrochemical phenomena going on ⋯ and when anything electrical is involved that means force fields. Electromagnetic fields are intangible – you can't reach out and grab a handful of that. You can't grab a handful of a gravity field either, but it's still very real to us, isn't it? We can witness the results; things fall down, they don't fall up. Electromagnetic force fields are very real too. Well, they play a role when thoughts bounce around in the brain. Now as a guy who has analyzed weak signals let me assure you that, whenever there are electromagnetic fields, there's radiation; there's propagation through space; those signals travel. Some people claim that they've tuned into that – and not all of them are faking it (*e.g.*, mother-to-infant). I hope that has taken some of the mystery out of it; we'll sidestep any question of how little power there really is here, what all is involved, how difficult it is to get the right tuning, etc. We don't have to know how much; all that's been established is that the notion of thought waves isn't some silly theory that only strange people believe – just as the experience of observing a TV image isn't restricted to strange people. You don't have to leave the physical realm to talk about that. Remarkable isn't the same as supernatural. Also, there's nothing inherently disturbing about something physical. How many times do scriptural passages refer to natural phenomena being used when there's no special requirement for something supernatural? Water, fire, hunger, thirst ⋯ natural occurrences, natural devices. The fact that these natural devices can be misused, and have been misused, is discouraging – even disastrous sometimes – but it doesn't mean that the device is intrinsically bad. After all, Who invented all this?

ENERGY FROM THOUGHTS - from FACT to FICTION

OK, there are weak signals going through space due to thoughts. Being electromagnetic, they travel at the speed of light – just as TV signals do. When a signal is sent from a TV transmitter in your town, it doesn't take long for you to pick it up. Just as radio waves travel over great distances – really really fast – thoughts can do that. Communications specialists analyze radio signals all the time, using all kinds of abstract concepts. But here's a *simpler* concept: imagine a tabulation with columns representing different people generating thoughts and rows representing different people who are the objects of those thoughts. So if I'm person *#43,753* and you're person *#17,862* then there could be a bin containing all my thoughts about you, in column *#43,753* and row *#17,862*. Within that bin we could imagine time markers for the date and the hour when each thought took place, and further subdivision into smaller bins for categories of happy thoughts, unhappy thoughts etc. ⋯ we can make this as detailed as we want; you get the idea. Extending that idea to include everyone would form an enormous table containing every thought ever conceived by all who ever lived (data base programmers would love this exercise). So far, no harm done; data bases shouldn't scare us, and there's nothing odd about energy associated with thoughts (Teilhard deChardin even ascribed some capacity to all cosmic matter, inanimate as well as organic). Well then, where's the problem? HERE'S THE PROBLEM: *attributing power and intelligence to the information itself or to the people who claim to access it for you – instead of recognizing God as the ultimate source of all intelligence and all power.* Pretty basic, huh? As

Sherlock might have said, Elementary, Watson. Isn't that more logical than imagining some abstract organism, called a universal mind, that supposedly owns this data base and can do great mysterious things with it?

There's a reason why I've gone to some effort to separate fact from fiction about thoughts travelling through space. The reason is that, for people who have witnessed or experienced anything resembling the power of suggestion, hypnotism, unexplained healing, telepathy, or anything you can't explain, you can come to terms with that without changing your faith. You *don't* have to sidestep Christianity and become a convert to mysticism or anything remotely related to it. Most people don't really understand TV. You didn't convert to mysticism because of TV signals, did you?

Another point: radiation from thoughts would be much weaker than TV − and therefore require more of what I earlier euphemistically called "tuning" to "the right wavelength." Those words are too simple; they don't really hack it. We're now talking about something that still makes sense *qualitatively* but it's more complicated than TV − enough for me to say that those trying to work with it the most don't fully understand it. To me that's a warning to go slow *if* you ever feel the need to understand it at all. You don't take your very first sailing lesson alone in a prototype experimental racing craft while blindfolded, over whitewater rapids during a storm. And, even if you do eventually reach some level of understanding about some unexplained experience, *never ever* lose your anchor. The power ultimately came from the same Creator that created everything else. What other explanation is there − that there was a Creator for everything *except* some universal mind, which has some kind of perpetual motion machine that somehow enabled it to build itself and make itself clever? C'mon. I'm not trying to discourage analytical investigation but let's not be preposterous while we're at it. Still the mirage persists. Some who really get into this psychic business revere that big database containing every thought ever conceived by everyone; it's owned by none and owned by all. It's the "Universal Mind" – the U and the M are capitalized to show some kind of reverence. Bah, humbug.

ENERGY FROM THOUGHTS
- WISHFUL THINKING

Now suppose you ignore what I just said and plunge into psychic efforts in a big way. Let's consider the possible consequences of sidestepping the logic. One way your efforts could turn out, of course, amounts to a complete lack of any visible success for all your work. Maybe you just can't get the method to work for you. When something like that happens, you feel that you've wasted your time.

The next question being brought up is: whether the power to influence events would be a good thing to have. Most of us would be tempted to take it if we could have it. But would it be good for us? Consider this example: you're someplace where a 50/50 raffle is being held. Suppose you had the power to rig the outcome and, somehow, you could do that in some way that didn't violate any code of ethics - so you win the 50/50 and your winnings come to $1000. You figure that's not a bad day's work, since it didn't take much effort on your part. Five minutes later a drawing is held for the door prize – a *million* dollars and your number is called. But you're ineligible because you won the 50/50. You sort of blew it, didn't you?

Actually, that kind of outcome is still a reasonably happy one; you still got a thousand dollar bonus. The real results might be a lot less benign than that. You might unleash forces that you can't control; there's any number of ways that our most careful schemes can backfire. The best laid plans of mice and men ··· etc. etc. etc.

Let's expand on that one a little. How much do you want to depend on some mundane thing you really don't understand? Suppose your computer one day stopped doing all the things it's been doing successfully for years. You tell a friend who takes your computer home for a day. The next day your computer works again, so you ask your friend, who says "I fixed it but I don't know what I did; I don't know why it works now." Would you be reassured? Another example: you insert a floppy disk and, PRESTO! your computer once again is humming along just like before there ever was a problem. But unbeknownst to you, that floppy disk had a virus set to go off next year. How do you know that you're not using something that has destructive power?

Even if no failures or disasters occur there's another, more insidious, possible result. One example of what I'm driving at now is a character named Craig Price in a book entitled *Poor No More* by the late Robert Ruark. This character grew up in a family of modest means and decided, at a young age, that he would become rich − and while he was at it, he'd be a ladies' man. It happened; the money fell into his hands and the women fell into his arms. The book didn't go into graphic detail about that; it was written before books became that way − but it doesn't matter here. The point is, this guy got pretty much what he wanted, when he wanted it. He just kept on racking up success after success. I guess you'd think this made him pretty happy, huh? That *poor slob was miserable*. At the end of the book, on his way back to some destination, he was wishing that he only *wanted* something. The last sentence in the book said something like "How very rich he would be, Craig Price thought, if he only had *something* − besides the million dollars waiting for him when he arrived." Left to our own designs, we could easily put ourselves into a trap.

THOUGHTS - ANYTHING ELSE ?

Sometimes there comes to mind an idea so completely out of character that we wonder how it ever happened. Walk by some bank and think about running in with a gun and robbing it plus everyone in sight – or something equally impossible. Some people call those off-the-wall thoughts their "demons" – and proceed to make the big mistake of worrying about them.

One of the best examples of carrying that process to extremes came in Dostoyevsky's *Crime and Punishment*. The main character had recurring thoughts about killing an old woman. He wondered about it, then he worried about it, and then allowed the thought to become a preoccupation. Finally, for no meaningful reason at all, he actually did it.

We don't have full control of what kinds of thoughts are initiated in our minds. We are able, though, to decide which thoughts are allowed to stay and which ones need to be rejected. Even if a thought we classified as unacceptable comes back repeatedly (like the tune of a song we actually don't like), we can keep classifying it as unacceptable. If we understand the process, we can also avoid worrying about it. Hey, whose mind is it anyway?

What's to be done about irrational thoughts? For starters, understand that they can often be traced, one way or another, to a hostile environment (such as our current "culture" of trash entertainment, etc.). Mentally assert your rights to your own mind. Throw away what you don't want, and don't allow it to worry you. There are more important issues to occupy your thoughts.

THE PURPOSE of DEFENSE IS to DEFEND

This is being written on Memorial Day, with thoughts of my brother and thousands more who, like him, did the hard part in a war. Carrying a rifle through difficult terrain and seeing friends become maimed, blinded, or killed is something I'm not qualified to describe. I do know that the U.S. comes up with the very best fighting troops − every time. Their grade: $A+$.

Another area where this author is unqualified to offer judgment lies in a second factor affecting defense: the political/administrative one. I have no authority and no desire to usurp any. Well, then, what *do* I have? Answer: information − about a third item in the overall picture − the defense industry. Allow me to jump ahead here to *our* grade: maybe C-. I can provide real-world examples and have done that − in print and in person, at various forums, for decades, all within the industry. Response: minimal, unsatisfactory; it's time to reach beyond the industry. The layman is entitled to know what follows.

Waste in DoD's budget now isn't due as much to fraud as to something more insidious − poor practices. Issues are subtle enough so that many of the industry's busy people are oblivious; they're smart enough to master the issues but lack the time to investigate. That seemingly incredible claim will not shock those aware of an obvious clue: follow-up contracts intended for fixes or improvements can be exploited beyond reason. Fix it, but not too well just yet. Above all, don't make it too easily fixable.

Imagine a salesman saying "You need new laces for those $80.00 shoes? That's another $80.00 − for each lace." No deal; everyone understands shoe laces. It's not that way, though, with complex electronic systems. Some at high levels, while "above the battle" technically, are nevertheless aware that something is very wrong. The night before 9/11/01 Defense Secretary Rumsfeld gave an (understandably forgotten, for now) ultimatum to the Pentagon – widespread superficial approaches are no longer acceptable.

This not-entirely-surprising situation has an outcome which, though self-evident, needs to be bluntly stated: While many in the defense industry try to do what's responsible, big-dollar contracts attract some whose only priority is financial. They move upward while 20-year-olds move horizontally – across the planet, putting their lives on the line when some of us won't risk our next promotion. What's the justification? None whatsoever, and there never will be any.

Some answers apply no matter where you stand. Advocates of social justice have long deplored the amount spent on defense. Whatever the merits or demerits of their position, one thing is clear – we can't afford to *waste* what is allocated toward defense. Whether the U.S. can't afford to increase or to decrease defense spending, it is clearly imperative to 1) spend wisely whatever budget is allocated, and 2) withhold advantages from potential future adversaries. ***That isn't happening.***

The status quo is patently unacceptable – utterly inconsistent with our 200-year history. Our existing defense equipment finds its way, via international markets, *to countries unencumbered by our self-defeating habits* while our new developments are compromised for profit. Why not give veterans' organizations a voice in decisions regarding exports? If the professionals

65

can't do it right, give a voice to those who shouldered the risk.

If common-sense steps were taken to counteract inferior practices, costs could be dramatically cut while performance could be markedly improved. Bureaucrats could also be relieved of pressure to spend whatever is allocated, often without a plan. Meanwhile, financiers can be blasted out of a profoundly disturbing preoccupation with the short-term and a blissful complacency about a supposed U.S. invincibility. If the "bottom line" is all that matters, then here it is: The way we're proceeding while smaller nations catch up on technology, it's only a matter of time before the U.S. suffers immense avoidable casualties in a high-tech war. The defense industry will then become a disgrace to every soldier who ever carried a rifle on foreign ground. The real "bottom line" isn't dollars but lives of troops.

There are enough individuals who acknowledge (privately, not yet publicly) what's been going on. They need to borrow a page from the play *1776*. The participants weren't at all perfect nor infallible, but they came together to produce a giant-sized result. The country now needs a giant-sized change in the defense business.

The subject line at the beginning of this discussion is now revisited. Why do we have a defense industry at all? Its purpose is not to build fortunes and careers. Eisenhower was right.

What does this have to do with Christianity? Answer: *stewardship*.

WHO'RE YOU CALLIN' STRANGE?

"God works in strange ways." How often have we heard that?

Wait a minute. Haven't we all had the experience of changing our mind about something after learning more about it? Was there anything we once dismissed as "strange" that later made sense? Prior to an event like that, whatever seems mysterious in our limited perception we call strange. Let's consider one of a zillion familiar examples: someone from a different country or from a different part of our own country speaks with an accent. We don't have an accent. What's "strange" is always whatever is over there somewhere else; never us. We flatter ourselves.

If we can misinterpret statements and actions of mere mortals, how much easier is it for us to misunderstand what an infinitely knowledgeable Divinity has planned? Did it ever occur to us that, once the complete set of facts comes to light, we might decide that it makes perfect sense after all? We might hit ourselves on the side of the head and say "Oh, so *that's* what was going on ··· ." Even if not, weren't we told that our best and brightest minds can hold just a small fraction of the Divine wisdom? There was never any guarantee that we could approach that level of brilliance.

Let's get with the program. God works in ingenious ways that we often don't understand.

WHAT'RE YOU CALLIN' a THREAD?

Think of a time when disaster seemed horrifyingly close, in time or distance of both. Then, with seemingly just a gnat's eyebrow to spare, the calamity was avoided. Your perception is that you came within a "smidgen" (or was that a microsmidgen? or a nanosmidgen?) of losing all. When that occurs we say that we were hanging by a thread.

We generally learn something important from an experience like that. Furthermore, what we learn is often indelibly implanted, precisely because of how close the disaster seemed to be. The same God Who spared you could also have prevented the scare, but maybe the scare was necessary for the learning experience. Maybe it was the lesser of two evils – a scare now isn't any great fun, but the future calamity that this lesson prevented would have been much worse.

Was that really only a thread holding back a catastrophe? Or, unknown to us, was it really in effect an invisible thousand-gage steel cable with 90-ton grappling hooks?

JESUS my LORD, my SAVIOR
– and my *COACH*

In practice one day, Ron missed a block. Immediately the coach decided to let Ron know what happens to running backs when a block is missed. He lined up the whole team in pairs and instructed each twosome, in sequence, to collide with Ron as he ran head-on toward us. I was in the next-to-last pair to "high-low" him and, as I said to my partner – "Ill hit him low; you hit him high" – we expected the threesome to fall in the direction we were running. It didn't turn out that way; I fell backward. Ron weighed only about 160 pounds but, evidently, that was 160 pounds of sheer determination. The coach looked at me, dazed on the ground, and said "Farrell, get up. I told you this was a rough game when you wanted a uniform."

The coach wasn't trying to be mean to me nor to Ron. His job was to make a team from a bunch of guys, by whatever means necessary. I needed to be more resilient. Ron needed to be more alert – and as a result, our running backs would have a more open field. Improvement all the way around.

Think of a time in your life when you had to endure an unwanted experience. You couldn't skip over it, slide under it, or go around it; as the saying goes,the only way out is through. Your Divine Coach was telling you "I know it hurts. Do it anyway. It will be better later – better than it would have been without the experience." How much later? How much better? Better in what way? All that varies with each individual case. But as you go through, know that benefit is really waiting for you later; that will make it easier.

69

DEJA-VU ?

In his early years one of the major ancient prophets (Isaiah) was becoming increasingly conscious of prevailing accepted life styles − and of the wide deviation from modes of conduct prescribed for God's chosen people. When the full realization hit him he was appalled. With the long and growing list of evils that plague our nation at this time, it seems unmistakable that the same logic applies to U.S. There is no need to reproduce that list here; the evils are self-evident and widely recognized.

What is *not* widely recognized, at least not thoroughly, is the threat implied by the presence of those evils. Therein lies potential disaster in multiple directions. Wake-up calls abound; the recent spectacular one (Sept. 11) is actually one of many. Somehow the full message didn't seem to penetrate enough, or wasn't remembered for a long enough duration. After a months-long period with outward expressions of patriotism and support, our *inward* attitudes and values have largely reverted to pre-9/11 form. Our trash culture continues almost uninterrupted, complete with export to other nations that hate us for doing the exporting. Whether we want to face it or not, that hatred fans the flames of violence. That's been stated and restated, in profuse recorded promises of revenge by inhabitants from diverse countries.

While reasonable people everywhere realize that terrorism can't be justified − and neither can hate crimes (which are futile anyway since they generally "retaliate" against an innocent majority) − an obvious accompanying fact often goes ignored or unresolved: Within the Islamic community, both the terrorists and the innocent majority observe a practice of multiple

70

prayer sessions daily. It is unrealistic to dismiss the innocent majority as fanatics; a great many of these people are devoted, and unwilling to hurt anyone for anything. They don't want violence any more than we do – and by praying several times daily they are doing something that most U.S. citizens aren't doing.

To those who see no connection with war, I can only refer to Biblical history. Every time ancient Israel fell into a familiar pattern (degraded values, widespread corruption, social injustice, etc.) that nation took punishment, big time. Sometimes calamity came as loss of a major battle. On rare occasions it was much more far-reaching – like the complete destruction of Jerusalem (*all* the buildings). Often the bad guys were used as agents handing out the punishment; that was allowed to happen. It came as no real consolation when those bad guys "got nailed" later; it didn't undo the harm to the earlier victims.

Various common-sense security measures are now being introduced. OK, but more is needed. For one item, there were interracial meetings during the late '60s and early '70s. Why aren't there Interfaith meetings all across the country today? More important, the next statement should probably be coming from an expert theologian instead of some layman with no credentials, but let's ignore the source and concentrate on the message:

> *What this country needs is a return to God, on a massive scale, by people from all walks of life regardless of color, creed, social and economic status, or any other variation.*

Skeptics are invited to review the historical records.

James L. Farrell

WHAT DO I KNOW ANYWAY ?

How many of us feel this way: Combine together what I've learned in a number of different areas. That might include a list something like this:

my own line of work

what is often very wrong with the way it is practiced in so many places

what is obviously very wrong with values prevailing in our "culture" today

how false values are successfully propagated, often accelerating through time

Scriptural warnings against much of what is accepted throughout our land

continuation of wrong practices, even after 9/11/01

All of this makes us feel as if we would be highly qualified to be featured speaker at graduation ceremonies and meetings of all types. Otherwise, why was I enabled to learn all this information?

Maybe we aren't really supposed to be representatives on any grand scale. One scriptural passage cautions "Not many ⋯ should be teachers ⋯ " − it could be that our assignment is to talk one-on-one, to one individual at a time. That doesn't translate into wasting what we've learned. Nothing is wasted if we accept its real purpose, often without knowing what that purpose is, where it will lead, or when, or even whether our interpretations will ever travel anywhere.

Information we have is a gift. It benefits us by natural psychological satisfaction derived from understanding issues and sharing our understanding with others. For many of us, that has to be enough; we were called on to be agents of little changes, not big ones.

#1 IS FIRST

Have you ever resented someone else taking credit for your work? Imaging trying to play that game against your boss. You might find yourself without a job. Now how about people playing that game against their *Creator* ? Not a good idea to risk that; the commandment involved here has a very significant number: one. Not a good sign if we don't even keep the very first rule.

Pretty obvious, huh? But what about all the practices – deemed "harmless" – widely accepted by a large majority of "civilized" society? Crystals. Astrology. Fortune-telling. Numerology. Various "new-age" concepts. Etc., etc., etc. Oppose those popular practices and you're labeled a fanatic. Ah, well – I oppose 'em anyway. It just really doesn't make sense to believe that celestial alignments or crystals (or anything that irrelevant) could exert rigid inescapable control over all details of my future. Nah. You don't have to be fanatical to reject illogical ideas. Nah.

THINK MENDELIAN GENETICS

The Serbs against the Croations. The Serbs plus the Croations against the Bosnians. The Irish against the English. The Catholic Irish against the Protestant Irish. The Israelis against the Arabs. The Greeks against the Turks. Or — from James Michener's *Hawaii* — the highland Chinese against the lowland Chinese plus the mainland Japanese against the Okinawans plus ⋯ . The list goes on and on. For a grand finale, Hitler's notion of a master race.

Although America has more work to do before we can claim to have social justice in all our race relations, we aren't alone when it comes to unnecessary conflict. Whoever started this hoax anyway — that ethnic purity in some one group will somehow produce superiority? It doesn't take any genius to see the contradiction: everyone can't possibly be better than everyone else. *Duh.*

Interaction, then, is essential to survival. That need for mixing isn't limited to talk. Plants benefit from cross-pollination. And *that* need for mixing isn't limited to plants.

I'm a half-breed who is glad not to be a pedigree. Look at what happens with in-breeding: big health problems of all kinds. Reasons were clarified through the concept of recessive genes. Now ask yourself — Who created the physiological system, and what do you suppose was the intention?

JUST in TIME for THANKSGIVING

A couple of decades ago someone else wrote a book with seven times as much information as this one − a brief essay for each *day* (not just one for every week). One daily theme in mid-November quoted a scriptural reminder from God. When a major problem presents itself − seemingly with no solution − the trouble may have been arranged by God Himself. Things happen for a reason; at times we may need to be turned (maybe unceremoniously) toward another direction. When that happens, accept it; do *not* complain.

I forced myself to be submissive when, exactly on the calendar date with that message, a major problem unexpectedly materialized. The situation was completely beyond my control and there was no apparent solution. More than a week of near-sleepless nights followed.

Over a week later that "daily message book" cited the passage from *Rom 8:28* about how all things work together for those ⋯ called to His purpose. The message went on to explain that this passage is not just speculation or a wish, but assurance. Reminders were offered about certain key words in the passage. For example, *work* isn't just luck or accidental. As another example, *together* doesn't mean isolated; one occurrence or one day's happenings alone won't provide a complete picture of a Divine plan.

In fact, one isolated incident might appear to be opposite the real situation. Sure enough, deliverance came − exactly on the date corresponding to that *Rom 8:28* passage. That doesn't mean these coincidences will always be evident but, in this case, the correlation seemed designed to offer a lesson to be absorbed.

IT'S the BERRIES

Cranberries on the turkey. Strawberries on the waffles. Blueberries *in* the pancakes. Raspberry sherbet. Blackberry jam (or blackberry brandy). All kinds of interesting uses for these little pieces of food.

It probably wouldn't be surprising to learn that berries perform some vital function in an overall ecological balancing act. Maybe some expert could show how, without berries, too many little creatures of a certain type would be deprived – leading to an oversupply of predators of some other kind, and on and on. There might have been a breakdown in the grand design of some botanical/organic universe (or whatever the right words are) if we didn't have berries. Even if that might be true, though, an infinitely intelligent Designer could undoubtedly have devised an alternative system able to survive without these little treats. With all the other treats already available, we might not have known the difference. Still, God chose to include those. Why?

Whatever the complete answer is, generosity probably had a lot to do with it. Like, here's a cake *and* here's icing on it. At the same time, it carries a reminder: We've gained from that generosity, so we should try to imitate it. Who is going without? Can we fix that?

In late 2004 the budget is being cut from the hugely successful <u>Food for Peace</u> program. After 50 years the U.S. lowers the priority of rescuing people in dire need. Imagine a shipwreck stranding all championship team members from the World Series and the Super Bowl, plus a world-class symphony orchestra. Then imagine a plan to rescue only the leaders, abandoning all others. Would that manager, coach, and conductor be showing leadership or misusing their privilege?

76

OPEN-SOURCE ANTIDOTE to a CLOSED POWER STRUCTURE

A contribution from my son, Michael Lawrence Farrell, in his third year as a computer science major at the time of this writing:

Today in many countries there are professionals in various fields (*e.g.*, medicine, technology, etc.) performing their work free of charge. The number of volunteers is impressive but still small in comparison to the need. Benefits of this activity include both internal satisfaction and outward philanthropy. Of course there is satisfaction from doing your chosen work correctly, unsupervised, by your own methods, and at your own pace. More important, the effort can provide a vital contribution. Millions of people in third world countries have hardly begun to benefit from today's modern advances.

In the field of computer technology, the concept of Open Source Software has gained considerable momentum in the past few years. Open source software, in brief, is distributed freely without any required compensation, financial or otherwise. Scientists in the field provide this work free of charge, releasing not only the finished product but also the underlying computer instructions (source code, closely guarded in most commercial environments). The basic premise of open source development is that scientific information should be public domain.

Implementing a concept of "scientific work as a hobby" (rather than a source of profit) can steer these benefits where they are most needed, often solving major

77

problems in the process. Some in the upbeat and rigorous computing field have been donating stable and efficient software for 5 to 10 years, with no regret for their give-something-back-to-the-world efforts. Why then can't the practice be spread? If those in need remember more of us as partners (rather than suppressors) in their learning experience, the power gained from that knowledge can be put to the best use.

MEANS of COMMEMORATION
– or SOMETHING ELSE?

Statues are all around us. When a park has a metallic or ceramic likeness of some past military or political figure, most of us see that as an effort to remind people of that individual's accomplishments or contributions. For other cases, though, perceptions can vary over a wide range. The point can be clarified if we consider, as an example, a statue of St. Paul. Respect for his writings would produce consistent positive reactions among most Christians – but a bronze or marble likeness of him would bring out disagreement.

To those who would condemn the existence of religious statues, one issue should not be hard to settle. No one in his right mind would really attribute any power to the inert object itself. The object itself isn't being worshiped or adored. That isn't – or at least shouldn't be – the argument. The real question is whether it is permissible to fabricate that likeness, as an object of commemoration or as an aid for focusing concentration during prayer. This writer won't presume to have the final answer, but attention has been drawn to a question of some significance.

Even without a definitive answer, it is possible to arrive at a recommendation. A reasonable solution is offered among the writings just mentioned. Specifically, note the principle applied to a completely different situation in *1 Cor 8:9, 8:13*. Even if we assume an action to be entirely permissible, those two verses make a case for forfeiting what is allowed. That conclusion seems especially significant in light of the strong and sincere opposition expressed by so many Christian denominations.

Christians everywhere understand that some day, somehow, there will be one fold and one Shepherd. Before that happens, there will probably be much negotiation to lessen the distance between various factions. Negotiations require concessions to succeed. Phasing out of religious statues would remove a major stumbling block.

FIGURING THINGS OUT

We know that God lavishes gifts for our own good —
many of those are spiritual gifts, aimed at eternity.
Then why does God so often give in to my *mundane*
desires and wishes? Especially when I didn't deserve
the favor? Some guesses:
  1) His unfailing generosity.
  2) It was good for my psychological health.
  3) He knew in advance I'd be grateful.
  4) He knew I'd be a witness to his generosity.
  5) Gratitude would prompt me to improve spiritually.

Maybe that last item is beginning to emerge. For more
years than I care to admit, my actions were aimed
toward becoming this or that (you know, some kind of
"wheel"). After enough humbling experiences
(becoming instead more like a hubcap) I finally asked
for a way for the outcome of those efforts (knowledge,
ability, contacts, etc.) to be salvaged — somehow — for
some Divine purpose (better late than never, even if
extremely late). It happens more often lately that what
I ask for will benefit someone other than myself, or
whole groups of others. That also increases my
confidence that the prayer will be answered in the
affirmative. Still, though, it's only a start — and fervor is
absent. Fervor is something I've read about, not
something I really know. So, once again, here goes
my excuse-making machine:

Lack of fervor isn't a reason to feel guilty. That
happens to the best of us (not that I would know by
myself but, fortunately, some of those best have
recorded their experiences so that the rest of us can
read about them). Often they just couldn't feel that
they were "in the zone" spiritually. OK, then, there
must be a way to make the best of the situation: Is it

possible that what I lack in fervor can be compensated for by correctness of intentions? Just as "the heart has reasons that reason knows nothing of" (Pascal), there could be another variation. I'm no Pascal but, when feelings confuse or fail to direct − as they often will − we might say that

Reason can "feel" direction that feelings know nothing of.

So there -- and you don't have to be an insensitive clod to believe that.

FIGURING SOME PEOPLE OUT

People often seem to have "their hearts in the right place" and, yet, many seem to attach low priority to God. How can that be? For one thing, scandals surely haven't helped; if some of the most visible representatives of religions do horrible things, they are doing a dismal sales job. In some cases it's just timing; think of your teen-age years. Preoccupation with everything tangible and/or delightful is long-lasting but still temporary. Don't assume someone is doomed for that reason; don't judge.

If we tend to compare our progress with the unenlightened, we're forgetting that we don't have a monopoly on Divine assistance. We need to be reminded that we don't really know who the unenlightened are, or how long they will stay unenlightened (we don't control their time-table).

Some Christians purposely limit their association to others who think the same way. They have their reasons, but that's not the way to spread the Word. It is widely known that, when Christ walked around on this planet, he didn't restrict His attention to the sanctimonious. Far from it; over and over His choice of associates would be called into question. It seems likely that, in His view, some "questionable" people had "their hearts in the right place" – and vice-versa (outwardly virtuous individuals had ulterior motives) – *sometimes* – again, don't judge (and don't generalize). Maybe we've had enough positive experiences to provide an anchor of stability and faith. If others haven't – yet – that could explain why some do desperate things.

83

HOW CAN I MAKE THEM UNDERSTAND?

An alarming number of people would acknowledge that they don't know God, or don't want to know God, or don't care. In many cases they once tried, maybe by asking Him for something, but later gave up. Among the various reasons are found some very familiar refrains, *e.g.*,

- all this "thee, thou, and thy" kind of talk is ancient and irrelevant now
- there was no visible response to their efforts
- there was no timely response to their efforts; far from it
- their needs weren't important enough for a response to be granted
- those who do profess to have faith set some terrible examples
- so many horrible things happen.

If one guy's testimony can count for anything, let me try to offset some of that skepticism. First, don't automatically count yourself out of this picture. If instead of "thee, thou, and thy" you talk in terms of bolts, screws, and wrenches – or old baseball stories, football scores, and slalom races – or boats, cars, the latest version of some software program or a hundred other things – fine; this is for you. Next let's consider whether there's any visible evidence of progress. When there isn't, never forget that big things can be happening behind the scenes. In fact, that's the way it usually works. So don't blow your chance by taking for granted that you can never have what you want.

Next step: Think of the most generous action you've ever heard of, then carry that example to the extreme, amplify it enormously, and expand that amplified result to a vast number of actions. Now add some caveats. In order to benefit from that generosity, you have to satisfy some requirements. First, don't try to demand a fix for everything that you think is wrong; give some focus to limited areas (in the beginning you might try one at a time) where you want to see a solution. You have to believe (or, for starters, at least admit the possibility) that the generosity – and the willingness to exercise it – are there. Furthermore it is accompanied by complete awareness of your specific situation, with an infinitely clearer understanding than your own. Then you have to make whatever efforts are called for by your needs. If you fail, get back up. While you're waiting, even if it's a very long wait, you need to acquire some patience; no grumbling. It might be wise to put some efforts into another area during a waiting period (*e.g.*,do some reading if you're recovering from surgery). You also need some flexibility; the outcome might contain some surprises, not exactly in line with your detailed specifications. Whatever happens, you won't be left empty-handed in the end. If you do it right, you might be astounded at the results.

Still unconvinced? Try it and see. What's there to lose except the habit of losing?

James L. Farrell

<u>CHRISTMAS</u>

On the street he envies all those lucky boys,
then wanders home to last year's broken toys
– The little boy that Santa Claus forgot, Connor/Leach/Carr
(J. Albert & Son)

That's from an old popular tune by Nat Cole. It's also a "chestnut" sung in four-part harmony. Barbershop arrangements span a broad diversity of themes. Down south. Here comes the choo-choo train. Songs about home, songs about mother. Funny songs, love songs, Irish songs, happy songs, exuberant (loud) songs ("gut busters"). And, yes, sad songs ("tear-jerkers"). As art imitates life, most any message of significance is present in the archives of barbershop.

The 51st week is of course the week of Christmas. A writing of this type therefore calls for something profound, original, eloquent, or at least noteworthy in some way. Lacking any of that capability within, this author is content to copy from other sources. There are means within reach that combine the Christmas spirit with helping the disadvantaged. We can't go wrong if we pursue this eminently practical approach:

On the website www.google.com, the combination "Christmas donation gift" produces about 140,000 responses. Among those can be found organizations with the specific purpose of replacing gift purchases by donations to a charity (for one of the many example descriptions, see www.barnardos.org.au). Many Americans rightly feel that they have been taken care of materially, especially in comparison to the less fortunate. Many have already made that substitution (Don't give me a gift; instead, help someone in need). What more can be said? *That's* Christmas.

THREE WISHES

The title above doesn't perfectly describe what follows, and what follows isn't a perfect way to conclude a writing of this type. In fact there is no perfect way to conclude this – and, if there were one, I'd be likely to miss it. Perfection doesn't seem to match me at all; in fact, that word hardly belongs on the same page as anything related to my name. Still, we have a clear directive from Scripture to aspire to perfection ("Be perfect, as your heavenly Father is perfect" – *Mt 5:48*). That's a tall order, especially for a guy like me; so now what?

Maybe I can begin by striving for complete conformance in certain areas.   Here are three possibilities:
- *Reverence.* As the heavenly Father is perfect, perfection calls for complete reverence. I know my place and, when trying to communicate with the Infinite, my place isn't at all a high one. In fact, I need to be like the one who "hardly dares to lift his eyes upward."
- *Submissiveness.* In asking the Almighty to maintain permanent full control over the events governing my life, I waive all claims to any rights or privileges associated with free will. If any steps I take are in the wrong direction, I ask to be overruled and reversed; clearly any guess I make is just a guess. I agree now to forfeit any future right to attempt any retraction of this commitment.
- *Gratitude.* If all blessings sent in my direction were to cease this instant, it would remain true that benefits already received have far outpaced any combination I could have anticipated. Years ago

if I could have been shown, in advance, all the good things to come, I would have been flabbergasted. I'm still flabbergasted now, looking back — and it isn't even over yet.

That's a start. Now as if to illustrate further my lack of perfection (4 is not equal to 3, and this page was identified as a list of three), a fourth item will be added: I won't give up trying to fix whatever else I'm handling wrong.